First World War
and Army of Occupation
War Diary
France, Belgium and Germany

52 DIVISION
Divisional Troops
Royal Army Veterinary Corps
1/1 Lowland Mobile Veterinary Section
1 April 1918 - 28 February 1919

WO95/2895/1

The Naval & Military Press Ltd
www.nmarchive.com
Published in association with The National Archives

Published by

The Naval & Military Press Ltd

Unit 10 Ridgewood Industrial Park,

Uckfield, East Sussex,

TN22 5QE England

Tel: +44 (0) 1825 749494

www.naval-military-press.com

www.nmarchive.com

This diary has been reprinted in facsimile from the original. Any imperfections are inevitably reproduced and the quality may fall short of modern type and cartographic standards.

© **Crown Copyright**
Images reproduced by permission of The National Archives, London, England, 2015.

Contents

Document type	Place/Title	Date From	Date To
Heading	WO95/2895-1		
Heading	52nd Division 1/1 (Lowland) Mobile Vety Section Apr 1918-Feb 1919		
War Diary	Sarona Jaffa	01/04/1918	02/04/1918
War Diary	Ludd	03/04/1918	04/04/1918
War Diary	Kantara	05/04/1918	06/04/1918
War Diary	Alexandria	06/04/1918	11/04/1918
War Diary	Marseilles	19/04/1918	19/04/1918
War Diary	Noyelles	20/04/1918	20/04/1918
War Diary	Romaine	21/04/1918	21/04/1918
War Diary	Grand Laviers	24/04/1918	25/04/1918
War Diary	Rue	27/04/1918	27/04/1918
War Diary	Aire	28/04/1918	28/05/1918
War Diary	Au Reitz Corner Mont St Eloy	01/06/1918	30/06/1918
War Diary	Au Reitz Neuville St Vaast	22/07/1918	31/07/1918
War Diary	Divion	03/08/1918	03/08/1918
War Diary	Ecoivres	04/08/1918	11/08/1918
War Diary	Breitencourt	29/08/1918	01/09/1918
War Diary	Boisleux Au Mont	04/09/1918	04/09/1918
War Diary	Croisilles	05/09/1918	05/09/1918
War Diary	Boiry	12/09/1918	12/09/1918
War Diary	St Leger	17/09/1918	17/09/1918
War Diary	Hendecourt	18/09/1918	18/09/1918
War Diary	Ecoust	28/09/1918	28/09/1918
War Diary	Morchies	28/09/1918	01/10/1918
War Diary	Moeuvres	07/10/1918	08/10/1918
War Diary	Manin	19/10/1918	22/10/1918
War Diary	Heninletard	24/10/1918	24/10/1918
War Diary	Warendin	28/10/1918	28/10/1918
War Diary	Beauvry	09/11/1918	09/11/1918
War Diary	Lacelles	10/11/1918	10/11/1918
War Diary	Herchies	11/11/1918	11/11/1918
War Diary	Baudour	30/11/1918	23/12/1918
War Diary	Casteau	31/01/1919	28/02/1919

(1) 10/2/95 8am

(1) 10/1/95 5am

52ND DIVISION

1/1 (LOWLAND)

MOBILE VETY SECTION

APR 1918 - FEB 1919

WAR DIARY or INTELLIGENCE SUMMARY

Army Form C. 2118

April 1918

Vol XX Page 1

1/1st (Lowland) Mobile Vety Section 52nd Div.

Place	Date	Hour	Summary of Events and Information	Remarks and references to Appendices
SARONA JAFFA	1-4-18		Handed over to 9th Indian Div. Mod. Vet. Sec. Proceeded with the Section to Surafend & camped	
"	2-4-18		Instructed to return to Sarona at above mentioned Camp.	
LUDD	3-4-18		Above all abovementioned Sec. Personnel phoned on all Vetn. horse & Remount Depot Lists.	
"	4-4-18		Entrained at Ludd 600 with 155th Inf Bde.	
KANTARA	5-4-18		Arrived Sidi's Camp Kantara.	
"	6-4-18		Entrained at Kantara 0100. Arrived at Alexandria Docks 1200.	
ALEXANDRIA	6-4-18 to 11-4-18		Embarked aboard H.M.T. "MALWA". 2 officers. 29 O.R.	
"	11-4-18		On board ship in Alex. Harbour.	
"			Convoy of 7 ships with escort left Alexandria Harbour at 1430.	
MARSEILLES	17-4-18		Disembarked at Marseille. Entrained at Marseille. 2 officers. 29 O.R. at 2300.	
NOYELLES	20-4-18		Detrained at Noyelles. Proceeded Billets at Romaine.	
ROMAINE	23-4-18		Drew 3 L.D. horses/mules & float from Adv. Horse Transport Depot. Abbeville	
GRAND LAVIERS	24-4-18		Section Complete moved down to GRAND LAVIERS	

J Mutchelow Capt AVC

VOL XX Page II

April 1918

WAR DIARY
INTELLIGENCE SUMMARY

1/1 (Low) Mobile Vety Section
52nd Div

Place	Date	Hour	Summary of Events and Information	Remarks and references to Appendices
GRAND LAVIERS	25-4-18		Received 16 Riders from Remounts	
RUE	27-4-18		Entrained at Rue 12noon.	
AIRE	28-4-18		Detrained at AIRE. Billeted in French Cavalry Barracks. Attached to XI Corps 1st Army. Received circulars & orders relating to Vety Services from D.A.D.V.S.	

J.B. Meikleham Capt A.V.C.
O.C. 1/1st Low. Mob. Vet. Sect.
52nd Div.

WAR DIARY or INTELLIGENCE SUMMARY

Army Form C. 2118

No 1 (Canadian) Mobile Vety Section

Vol XXI Sheet I

Place	Date	Hour	Summary of Events and Information	Remarks and references to Appendices
Aire	1/3/18 2/5/18		Completed equipment. Received & evacuated 12 animals to V.E. h, Vet Evacuating Station AIRE.	
	3/5/18		Received instruction to move with Hrs. to An Reilly Corner. Advance party proceeded by train.	
	4/5/18		Proceed by march route. Camped at — DIVION.	
	5/5/18		Continued march to AV REITZ CORNER. Took over M.V.S. from 4th Canadian Div M.V.S.	
	13/4/18		Mob. Vet evacuation Station in district. Evacuated 23 animals by rail to Aulnoye Mob Vet Evacn Station.	
	14/5/18		Received notification that XVII Corps M.E.S. was to be moved to EQUIHEN. Evacuated 20 animals to 13 V.R. Athenville.	
	16/5/18		Notified that XVIII Corps M.E.S. would open on the 20/5/18.	
	17/5/18 18/5/18		Received notification from XVIII Corps that 2nd & 5th AVC men to XVII Corps V.E.S.	
	19/5/18		1 O.R. proceeded on leave to U.K. S.O.R. Lieut to 18th V.E.S. & struck off strength & posted to XVIII Corps M.V.S. I.O.R.	
	20/5/18		1 O.R. proceeded on leave to U.K.	
	24/5/18 25/5/18		Sent Vet state D.A.&Q.M.G.	

Army Form C. 2118

1/1 Canadian Mobile Veterinary Section WAR DIARY
or
INTELLIGENCE SUMMARY
(Erase heading not required.)

Vol. XXII
June 1918

52

Instructions regarding War Diaries and Intelligence Summaries are contained in F. S. Regs., Part II. and the Staff Manual respectively. Title Pages will be prepared in manuscript.

Place	Date	Hour	Summary of Events and Information	Remarks and references to Appendices
Au Reitz Corner Mont St. Eloy	1/6/15 to 30/6/18		Evacuated 17 animals belonging to various Divisions during the month. Major J. Adamson M.C. ave DADVS returned from leave on the 19/6/18 & I relinquished the duties of DADVS on this date. There is nothing further of interest to report.	

B Maclachlan
Captain V.C.
OC 1/1 Can Mob Vet Sect

Army Form C. 2118

WAR DIARY
or
INTELLIGENCE SUMMARY

19 1/1 Lowland Mobile Vety Sect

Vol. XXIII

July 1918

(Erase heading not required.)

Place	Date	Hour	Summary of Events and Information	Remarks and references to Appendices
AV REITZ NEUVILLE ST VAAST	29/4/18		Received instruction to proceed north M.V.S. by road to Lewin	
	2 3/9/18		Proceeded to Lewin	
	3/4/18		96 Animals evacuated during month through 162nd V.E.S. FREVIN CAPELLE 14 through 13th V.E.S. PERNIES.	

R. M. Walker
Captain

29-9 Vol XXIV Sheet one

WAR DIARY or INTELLIGENCE SUMMARY

(Erase heading not required.)

Army Form C. 2118

AUGUST 1915

1/2 Lowland Mobile Vety Section

Vol 4

Place	Date	Hour	Summary of Events and Information	Remarks and references to Appendices
DIVDM	2/8/15		Received instructions to proceed to ECOIVRES by road.	
ECOIVRES	4/8/15		Temper to visit the 1st Canadian M.V.S. Evacuated animals kept.	
"	11/8/15		Proceeded on 14 days leave to the U.K. Capt Kerr was taking charge of the Section during my absence	
BRETENCOURT	29/8/15		Returned from leave. Evacuating animals through the XVII Corps. M.V.S. at BEAUMETZ.	

B. Maclachlan Captain.

O.C. 1/2 Lowland M.V.S.

1/1st Lowland Mobile Vety Section

WAR DIARY
or
INTELLIGENCE SUMMARY

Army Form C. 2118

VOL XXV / Sheet 1

SEPTEMBER 1918

Vol 5

Place	Date	Hour	Summary of Events and Information	Remarks and references to Appendices
BRIETENCOURT	1/9/18		Proceeded to Boisleux-au-Mont	
BOISLEUX-AU-MONT	4/9/18		Proceeded to CROISILLES	
CROISILLES	5/9/18		Proceeded to BOIRY	
BOIRY	12/9/18		Proceeded to ST LEGER	
ST LEGER	17/9/18		Proceeded to HENDECOURT	
HENDECOURT	18/9/18		Proceeded to ECOUST-ST-MEIN	
ECOUST	20/9/18		Proceeded to MORCHIES. Camped in a German Field Ambulance	
MORCHIES			Number of animals evacuated during month 364.	

R. Mackellar Capt & ??
O.C. 1/1 Lowland Mob V.S.

Army Form C. 2118.

WAR DIARY
or
INTELLIGENCE SUMMARY.
(Erase heading not required.)

No 1 Mobile Veterinary Section

OCTOBER 1918.

VOLUME XXVI.
SHEET 1.

Place	Date	Hour	Summary of Events and Information	Remarks and references to Appendices
MORCHIES	1/10/18		Section proceeded to MOEUVRES.	
MOEUVRES	7/10/18		Relieved by M.V.S. 24 & this. Proceeded to RIVIERE GROUVILLE	
	8/10/18		Continued march by road to MANIN.	
MANIN	19/10/18		Proceeded to ECOIVRES.	
	22/10/18		Continued march to HENIN LETARD.	
HENIN LETARD	24/10/18		Proceeded to WARENDIN.	
			Proceeded to BEUVRY	
WARENDIN	31/10/18		Number of animals evacuated during month 140.	

J Mackechlan
Capt A.V.C.
O.C. No 1 MVS

Army Form C. 2118.

WAR DIARY

1/1st Lowland Mobile Veterinary Section

INTELLIGENCE SUMMARY

November 1918.

Vol XXVII Sheet 1

Place	Date	Hour	Summary of Events and Information	Remarks and references to Appendices
BEAUVRY	9/11/18	—	Moved to LACELLES. Camped overnight	
LACELLES	10/11/18		Moved to HERCHIES do	
HERCHIES	11/11/18		Moved to BAUDOUR. Received instruction that hostilities would cease at 1100	
BAUDOUR	30/11/18		Animals evacuated during Nov. 1918 — 103	

J.J. Mackechnie
Captain

Army Form C. 2118.

WAR DIARY
or
INTELLIGENCE SUMMARY.

Vol. XXVII
1/1st Lowland Mobile Veterinary Sec.
Sheet 1.   DEC. 1918

(Erase heading not required)

Place	Date	Hour	Summary of Events and Information	Remarks and references to Appendices
BAUDOUR	23/12/18		Section moved to CASTEAU. Sheet 45. K.11.8.2.	
			Number of Animals evacuated for Month of Dec 103.	

A. Whitelock
O/C 1/1st Lowland Mob Vet Sec
Capt R.A.V.C
O/C 1/1st Lowland Mob Vet Sec

WAR DIARY or INTELLIGENCE SUMMARY

Army Form C. 2118

V°/XXIX/1st Lowland Mobile Vety Sect

JAN 1919

SHEET 1

No 9

Place	Date	Hour	Summary of Events and Information	Remarks and references to Appendices
CASTEAU	31/1/19		Section remained at Casteau during the month	
			Number of animals evacuated during month 204	

J.D. McLachlan
Capt. RAVC
O.C. 1/1st Low. M.V.S.

Army Form C. 2118.

WAR DIARY
or
INTELLIGENCE SUMMARY.

(Erase heading not required.)

1/1 Lowland Mobile Vet Sect

Vol 1

Place	Date	Hour	Summary of Events and Information	Remarks and references to Appendices
Casteau	28.2.19		Section remained at Casteau during the month.	
			Number of Animals Evacuated during the month 194	
			A sale was held at SOIGNIES on the 28/2/19 when 103 animals were disposed of.	

J.G. McLintockson
Capt R.A.V.C.
OC 1/1 Lowland M.V.S.

www.ingramcontent.com/pod-product-compliance
Lightning Source LLC
Chambersburg PA
CBHW051528190426
43193CB00045BA/2654